THE PAINTER
ON HIS BIKE

First published in 2019 by
The Dedalus Press
13 Moyclare Road
Baldoyle
Dublin D13 K1C2
Ireland

www.dedaluspress.com

ISBN 978-1-910251-62-1 paperback
ISBN 978-1-910251-63-8 hardback

Dedalus Press titles are available in Ireland
from Argosy Books (www.argosybooks.ie) and in the UK
from Inpress Books (www.inpressbooks.co.uk).
Printed in Ireland by Digital Print Dynamics.

Cover photograph: 'Grafton Street Cloud'
by Mark Granier, by kind permission.

The Dedalus Press receives financial assistance from
The Arts Council / An Chomhairle Ealaíon.

THE PAINTER
ON HIS BIKE

ENDA WYLEY

DEDALUS PRESS

ACKNOWLEDGEMENTS

Acknowledgements are due to the following publications in which a number of these poems, or versions of them, originally appeared: *The Irish Times, Poetry Ireland Review*, ed. Eavan Boland), *New Hibernia Review, The Well Review*, ed. Sarah Byrne), *Writing the City* (Dublin's Culture Connects, 2018), *Reading the Future; New Writing from Ireland*, celebrating 250 years of Hodges Figgis, ed. Alan Hayes (Arlen House, 2018), *Metamorphic, 21ˢᵗ Century Poets Respond to Ovid*, ed. Nessa O'Mahony and Paul Munden (Recent Works Press, 2017), *The Enchanting Verses Literary Review*, ed. Patrick Cotter (2016), *makebelieve* with the support of ID2015, ed. Roger Bennett (2015), *Once Upon a Place*, ed. Eoin Colfer (Little Island, 2015), *World English Poetry*, ed. Sudeep Sen (2015), *Berryman's Fate: A Centenary Celebration in Verse*, ed. Philip Coleman (Arlen House, 2014).

The following poems were commissioned for arts projects and broadcast on the cited programmes: 'The Painter on his Bike' was commissioned by Dublin's Culture Connects for The National Neighbourhood Project 2017–2108 and was displayed in Aungier Street, Dublin, 2018. The poem was broadcast on *The Culture Cabinet* RTÉ Radio 1 December, 2018, read by artist James Hanley and was also read by the author on the poetry podcast, *Words Lightly Spoken*, 2019. 'Home' was written for a film-poem with the artist Anita Groener for The Bealtaine Festival, 2018. 'Time Capsule' was written for *The People's Acorn / Dearcán na nDaoine* for Áras an Uachtaráin by artist Rachel Joynt. 'On Friendship' and 'Private Space' featured on Lyric Poetry Files, Lyric FM in association with Poetry Ireland, 2017. 'Coming Storm' was broadcast on *Sunday Miscellany*, RTÉ Radio 1, 2018.

I am indebted to The Tyrone Guthrie Centre, Annaghmakerrig, where several of the poems gathered here were written and revised. Thanks to Pat Boran and Raffaela Tranchino at Dedalus

Press. Much gratitude to Peter and Freya Sirr, Rachel Joynt, Anita Groener, James Hanley and Bernadette Larkin for their inspiration and support.

Contents

NOTES / 62

for Freya
& Peter

The Painter on his Bike

for James Hanley

balances his father –
sketched in pencil –

wrapped in paper
on his handlebars.

As he cycles down
Heytesbury Street

the twist of string
around the frame

loosens for a second
catches in the wheel

the painter's breath
caught too

by the sudden sight
of his dead father's eyes.

They saw me
before I saw myself …

He stops at the kerb,
tugs at the twine, frees it

from the spokes, sets off
again, the bike wobbling,

bumping over
potholes and tramlines,

the picture beating
against his knee.

He is cycling
the portrait home.

And later, a fire lit,
the paper unbound –

Father, whose eyes
rise up, from the face

your son drew,
like two dark lost moons.

There We Were

for Lainey

There we were
where winter

was a splinter
of sun

through the roof
of our thirty years

where days
were a puzzle

like the scratching
of city rats

in the old
house walls.

We could have stayed
forever

but then
the bells rang

our floors shook
and we were saved –

peered out to see
spring swagger

up from the river
in a cape of light

our future
a new cathedral

to enter
and to claim.

Solar Eclipse

for Janet Mullarney

Take a chance. Knock. You might be
let in through that wooden door.

Step carefully but do not be afraid.
He only wants to startle you –

peacock on the kitchen floor,
who flew from Ravenna

and landed here, to strut
below the pomegranate tree.

Indigo blue and emerald green,
this bird of linoleum marquetry –

his eye a fallen fruit, ruby red,
curious within his tiny head.

Take a chance. Go there so you may
know the quiet square, the white door

and how, after the moon has passed
between sun and earth,

sudden light will strike
the lamellae of this bird –

a thousand coloured spots
shimmering on the kitchen floor.

Safe

for Jenny Murphy

That you be safe
that we all sit close

this late July morning
at the kitchen bench

that there be
an abundance of grapes

in the heat of the artist's
conservatory

that berries
be plucked and preserved

and that coffee should flow
like our banter

that we stand together
on the grassy lane

see Hannah
ramble down

from her cottage again
a summer ghost

and that we remain
secure

as the post office safe
robbed years ago

ransacked and dumped
beyond in the ditch

far away from that chase
still enduring there.

Diptych

1. COCKEREL

in memory Dennis O'Driscoll

It was the painter
brought me back to you,

who sneaked into
the crowded gallery room

not wanting to paint
but to watch *him* paint

all the children there
and you too old for the class

but not too old to care
how first he orders the page

segmenting it into squares,
then forms with his palette knife

the surprise of a cockerel's head,
his oils spilling such defiant colours

that they unsettle your day,
your winter coat twitching

in a cruel December wind.

2. COMING STORM

after the painting by Martin Gale

What hopes we had
but any second now the rain –

ditches flooding, the lost field
waterlogged, the straggly hills

barely seen beyond the barrier
of drenched trees.

What hopes we had, the marquee
pegged into the ragged high grass

of late summer joy but billowing
with a wind that flattens all promise.

And any second now rain from the grey
eye of clouds that gather on your canvas.

You step back from the oils' secrets,
pace your studio, think even the sturdy Jeep

has no strength to save this tent,
striped and tensely pitched to be levelled,

folded up, dispensed with until another year
comes around again – when life, the show, goes on.

Pygmalion

after Joseph Walsh's Magnus Modus, The National Gallery

And in the end it is this that I return to –
thing of my own making that loops upwards

like branches thirsty for light, reaching high
to the glazed roof where the river gulls balance

close to the city's slate-grey sky. Listen now:
how they scratch and squawk their racket of desire

but they will never rest or nest in my carved olive ash.
In the long courtyard below four vast windows

have opened again to light that floods the walls
of white ceramic tiles, floods my graceful looping art

that I go back to in the end, ascending with it,
rising to sun, rising to shadow, all life there

in its smooth wood that night beckons me to touch.
Then it is woman, her skin beneath my thumb soft as wax in heat

and I gather marigolds for her, burn incense at her tiny feet, sing
sweeter than Orpheus ever did, press a ring upon her every finger

and, in the early hours, leave feverish for nightfall again –
our love renewing itself, assured as tomorrow's wedding bells.

Postcard to a Piper

for David Power

And so, where are you now?
It's days since your chanter let loose

its wild talk with the fiddle, days since
that early June night when all became

flow and speed and noise and slow,
the fiddler's eyes opening at last

from his own trance of melancholy
to reels that went so fast, that caught our hearts

twisting them into elation, then lifted us up
to a straight-backed ovation.

Back then, not even a short respite, the cool
of damp grass against our ankles, not even

the bitter wine could have distracted us.
We would go on with you for hours, to where

I see you now; crossing the fields,
air passing through your pipe's reeds,

a dream spilling out onto the dry land,
made abundant again with each step

towards me, waiting there for your song
in the dark, before you wake again to a hall

of light, before everyone, everyone applauds –
the tangle of night unravelling its secret tune.

At Rosses Point, Yeats's Cat

for Margaret Kelleher and Lucy McDiarmid

That you would come so effortlessly,
a cat rubbing its back in the misty grey

against the low wall at Rosses Point –
so lost, so in need of affection you looked

that we stopped our car and crossed
the sea road to sit and pat you there.

Queen Méabh's nipple was absent in cloud,
and night came upon us fast while our camera

caught you, Minnaloushe, slinking against
our backs and now suddenly alive, dancing

in the yellow light, lifting to the shifting
moon your changing eyes, burning, wise –

while we stayed put, transfixed, vowing
not to climb Knocknarea that night.

Time Capsule

Rachel Joynt's Acorn Sculpture with Time Capsule Writings,
Áras an Uachtaráin.

There's a canister made of steel.
The sculptor has spent long months

imagining it, then cast it in bronze,
a time capsule dug into the heart

of an acorn, balancing it at last
in these tree-filled grounds.

Our words have no rules,
unloose themselves within

this vessel, are floating free.
To live in a double decker bus!

Go mbeidh gach duine sláintiúil …
And listen, Emmanuel walks

with his dad to Doughiska; *We talk*
and I feel like life is great.

So much history carried forward
to another time, when a gloved

hand reaches up, one hundred years
from now – a cold November day

that we will never wake to –
and unlocks the sealed case,

24

our unearthed wishes
soaring on paper wings.

To the Core

remembering Helen Dunmore

Even when the anaesthetist
is in the ante room about his business

you are a poet to the core
in the way you feel the rhythms

of life must go on beyond this moment
and yet because of this moment.

A poet to the core, you see that all of us
are inside the eternal wave that rolls us

forward, though we move with it only for
our brief time. A crash and then we're gone.

Eurydice Speaks

At the edge of my new life, in the early hours,
a message comes to me: *Follow the passage*
of light up to your old world and stop halfway.

I don't understand why, but I do it –
walk and walk, then wait in that strange
space that's divorced me from you.

And waiting alone, I feel nervous like when
I'd been human and you'd run your hand
for the first time gently down my throat,

down from the tip of my chin through the valley
of my breasts to that dark place below my navel,
which I remember allowing only you to find.

The tunnel's midway point charges with your energy
and I realise I've been given a second chance –
sent here to catch one more sighting of you, up ahead.

I'd know your back anywhere, the fallen coat hem
that I'd promised to stitch – too late, the snake
took me from you – your face resolutely forward,

your shoulders hunched in the uphill climb.
I trace your footprints marked in damp clay,
softly follow them. I can wait for you.

The light ahead will make me woman again.
But you haven't changed. The warning's ignored;
your impatience takes over. You turn around your face

and I can't help it, cry out, immediately become shadow,
a ghost of a song you'll sing forever. You can't return twice
to where you found me. One look from you and I know this.

First Woman

in memory Janet Armstrong

The heart has a finite number of beats –
so why waste time? Better look to the moon
and go there, is what you thought, never said.
But I always knew this is what you wanted
to do, when we lived in the cabin high in the hills
with no water or heating, just our stoic unison
that never failed us, giving little away to others
about what we felt. Only our daughter dying
at three weakened our resolve, yet still we went on,
our small steps, your giant leap onto the unknown
lunar surface, the whole world watching, our sons
and I holding our breaths until you came back
to incubation, isolation, and our eventual
separation – silence your only answer.

Home

for my parents

If I could go back, it would be to there –
early summer and I would be barefoot,
the line of hot tar in the middle of the road
bubbling under my toes, the tree's blossoms
a spread of pink below our bedroom window.

There's the squawk of gulls rising up
from the fish at Dún Laoghaire pier,
the squeal of children leaping over
the hedge nets of back garden play –
The more you eat, the more you jump …

There's the sun through the kitchen window,
glinting on my mother's hair;
she swivels from a full sink,
scattering suds and laughter
as she bends to me.

If I could go back, it would be to there –
those rooms, the smell of dinner.
Key in the lock, our father calls, *Home …*
Night bringing its skillet of dreams,
our ticking clock wound tight.

Ledger

for Peter Sirr

In the attic dark the red box
that's waited for years to be
hauled down into the light again.

Standard Feint, yellow notebooks
of your past, all dusty – your ancient longing
made real with the swipe of cloth

and those poems you wrote still there
from when you'd first imagined them.
Frantic ink of desire.

How you ran through the snow to lose her,
unlearning her name to find her again in days
of bed and feasts of wine, nights of Callas –

unending light, unending splendour
that I later reached for on the bookshop shelf,
knelt to read in the hush of the poetry corner.

Her alabaster breasts, his querulous stare
and poised quill, her gentle hand on his
velvet blue jacket – that cover, your book

trembling in the palms of my hands,
this ledger of lost love I'd never read before
that thrilled, made me stand up in the bookshop,

then make for the door, our future racing out onto
Dawson Street and into the city's expanse,
Larkin raising his hands to me, the gulls cawing

encouragement as I sought you out, your face staring
from a high window over Parnell Square, the life
you'd described becoming ours, the door unlatched.

Mirror,

framed in slate, bought years ago in Mother Redcaps
when I'd climbed the hill to the cathedral bells,
spied you rummaging at the market stalls for that
first gift for me – engraved with *Moon Child* –
still reflecting this changing face.

Coin on the palm of the fortune teller, our daughter
rising from the tarot, the dusty velvet curtain pulled
back to declare our future – us weaving our way into
the city's black pit, finding comfort in darkness,
in the clink of a yard gate, the green chipped door.

What we want is the familiar, the din
of what we were, and you walking towards me
from old macramé lampshades,
battered chairs, glass necklaces tinkling as you pass.
The spiced air expectant. My full face rising to you.

Tree House

for Freya on her Birthday

Today you've a stove blazing
in the tree house beyond Cliffony.

The floorboards are swaying
as you toss, then rise.

Day of bluebells and wild garlic,
of the willow heart nailed to the red door.

Rain will fall but the walls within
are plum-red and warm blankets

protect you. The future's content –
a dog dozing on a sheepskin rug

and on the counter, a wicker basket
filled with everything you'll need.

Black Rocks, Derrynane

What brings us back to these black rocks –
marked with gulls' white guano –
that slope to murky pools of sea lettuce
and lime star shapes I try but can't name?

What brings us back to bladderwrack,
its secrets bulging on these black rocks,
as we clamber on, slip a little, stop
in small hollows of warm-white sand

where sated birds drop crab shells
the sand mites burrow to but we crush
underfoot, wincing at summer's sharpness.
What brings us back to these black rocks?

Is it that day we scramble to, when we made
these ink-dark rocks our picnic base, spread out
a late July feast, our future distant as Beara
and us laughing, younger, sunburnt and not caring?

Or is it our daughter we climb to now, a beacon
in an orange jacket, luminous fun at the sea's edge
spread-armed and dancing, chanting her rhymes
to the salty air? She has made this place her own –

is oblivious to us far back on these black rocks
we falter over, are cheated by, time pushing us away
and though we call out her name, she doesn't see
how we slip away from her, as our parents did from us.

Speed's Map

That was the day
I sped over
Harold's Cross Bridge,
Speed's map of Dublin
newly framed and rattling
in my bike's basket –

his yellow streets
a secret present planned
while you lay soaked
in fever that I would
soon succumb to too.

But at that moment
I could only think
of the thrill
of Christmas morning,
and you rustling the gift alive –

a slight mud splatter
on the frame, a tiny chip
where a pebble sliced
the thin glass.

Minor details, really –
who would care
why they were there?
But I did and still do.
The too fast race of me to you.

Red Mouse

You ask for your navy ink pen,
your notebook – oh, and the red mouse.

I imagine it, nestling in the pages
of the spiral-bound notebook,

see it now nibbling its way
through scribbles thin as its tail

breakfasting on troubadour songs
or dialogues from your play.

But I find instead a red plastic device
snug in the palm of my hand,

small enough to wrap amongst your
clothes, the hospital corridor white

and endless as an airport's,
though there is no plane to catch –

only you, resting behind curtains, marking
words on a screen, the red mouse sliding

over the pale blue blankets of the ward,
your fingers deleting illness with a click.

Walks

IN SILENCE WE WALK

This day our best conversation.
There is no need for words –
only your hand smooth in mine
like the pebble I'll skim across the river.

LANE

On the lane to Rath I see you now,
illness a coat tossed over the hedgerow –
and you striding into evening's soft relief.

Short Love Poems

1. LATE STAGE

I was wrong to think
it didn't matter –
the heaviness
of your hand
on my hip,
or your constant
late night breathing.

Wrong to think
that the poem be never made
again, or that you might not
reach for me once more
at this late stage.

2. LULLABY

Pillow that holds your scent still, magnesium
that will open my heart to you. I let night's stubble
brush against my chin, feel sleep kiss my forehead.
I wait for you – your voice a lullaby on the air …

3. AFTERWARDS

Morning gave us the bitter taste
of lemon water, taught us to stretch
like planks on the green wooden floor,
sent the crazed spaniel to scratch
at our bedroom door, made us all
frantic to get out on the long beach
and solve the riddle of wild pools –
how to cross over, what might come next?

Last night we'd talked the dark away,
and afterwards, our time together
felt delicate; hung like a tiny red
coral ball on the day's silver torc.

From the Archives

for Tom Quinlan

And here is the Keeper, carefully
bringing you to me,
crossing the hundred years between us.

He slides open the wide drawer,
spreads your files
on the long table high over Dublin:

young men just freed from childhood,
anxious in grainy black and white.
Larceny, drunkenness, the prison papers say.

There's the smell of hops; horses clatter
through the Coombe. From the stinking markets
the ghost of a woman rises,

fish oil on her hands.
She is making for home
where she eats a stolen pig's tongue,

eases herself into the creaking leather
of a mahogany chair
also stolen, then waits

head cocked for the violent rattle
at the tenement door,
the peeler standing red-faced before her.

Light On

I go to the city
to look for you,
stand on the pavement

opposite the gallery
and peer up
at the tall windows

that face the old hotel,
just want to stand here,
my face raised

to where I know
your desk has been,
one floor over the paintings

the buyers have come to view,
two floors above
the street noise

that now and then
distracted you from work,
your pencil cast aside

the page
an incomplete building,
the thin rectangles

of glass not yet drawn
on the white walls in your head.
And I expect nothing this night

just after the summer solstice,
the June sun
still bright, intense,

want only to stand here
as if this old house is enough –
searching for a light

that I see now.
Is it the sky's reflection,
its orange hue,

or might it be you,
all the time waiting?
Lift the sash window up,

breath of fresh air
ours again, the past
returned to, welcomed.

Winter Solstice

Why Go Bald flashes
above our heads,
the buses swing
onto Dame Street,
and the sculptor's chair
torn down years ago
is, for us, still there
in the vacant lot,
its perfect back
a tree blooming
inside our heads
as we lean into
bicycles, lean into
each other, our day
stretching into dark.

There has been sun –
shaft at dawn
through the roof box
lighting the chamber
we crawled down
the mysterious passage to.
But for now, this night
like a blanket
drawing us closer –
people slipping by
in the evening rush,
not noticing us,
lost in this time
we have made our own –
our mouths tilting
on their own axes
towards a new solstice.

Portobello Bridge Revisited

in memory of Pearse Hutchinson, 1927 – 2012

Coming over Portobello Bridge
I think of you swaying on the upper deck
of the bus, your boyhood perched there
just beyond St Mary's playing fields,
the surprise of a poem in your pocket,
the stretch of the long road behind you –
swimming pool, coffee shops, *Umi* –
and Dublin's mountains snow-cold,
watching you rise over the canal,
while your stomach flips up to your heart
that swells at the thought of the city ahead.

Up and over, then down Aungier Street,
and through the breath-fogged windows
of that upper deck, you know that this is life –
that excitement lies ahead, your seat creaks
as you stand, balance on a slate grey aisle,
holding tight to a yellow pole until it's time.
Then the stairs twist you down,
you are pushed out onto the pavement –
early morning crowds, a cavalcade of cyclists
to escort you, the traffic lights change
to green. The day says, *Go!*

Calling on a Friend

I go to my friend, we walk on the grass,
And the hours and moments like minutes pass.
— Stevie Smith

It doesn't matter that you're not here –
enough the dogs bark when the old gate creaks,
enough I imagine you, *hello, hello,* unlocking the door,
house light falling through the half-moon fanlight,
the letter box and door saddle rattling a welcome

to me standing on the steps, wanting to talk
with you under the copper leaves of a Japanese maple …
years of knowing one another … the world beyond
shrinking and just us here. It doesn't matter
that you're not home; I'll call again.

On Friendship

for Jacinta Wright, 12 May 1966 – 3 January 2015

I wake with eyes red from late night wine,
you twisted in blankets, the dog shifting
under the oak xylophone, notes rising delicately.

I wake to what has gone –
too much laughter and not caring,
too much not knowing and better that way.

Friends have been felled like magnificent trees
and sadness overwhelms when least expected
like standing at the edge of a noisy street

but in my head only silence.
When to cross, which way to go –
it becomes too difficult to decide.

Someone is hailing a taxi,
a bus is a wind braking under the green trees.
Where and when we live is not important – but how.

Woodbank Revisited

for Lynda

The avenue forever leading to here –
lamb roasting in the Aga, the washing dried
on racks your mother roped, cigarette slanting
at the side of her mouth, up to the high ceiling.

And outside, the garden of secrets –
those basement windows opening
to banks of woods over the bay,
our whispering hide and seek.

Now an ageing has come, that leads us to this –
the old house sold, your parents haunting it.
There's a whiff of elsewhere in the corridors,
an eerie wind bursts open a long locked door ...

The past's avenue reaches us here, the clatter
of jokes and rows, unending laughter –
and look, your dog Juno bounds from her
grave, licks our open hands.

Ghost Message

The window sprung open for no reason
and then I saw what I hadn't before –
the tall glass with its chipped plum frame,

the beam of age traversing the granite wall,
the way light played with the afternoon wind
and how ivy scurried across the old cottage beyond.

A hand not there, a person unseen, the window
sprung open for one reason – that I should see
what I hadn't before, get up and go outside.

Private Space

Annaghmakerrig

I went to your room when you'd gone –
was nervous turning the mahogany handle,
thought some ghost of a hand might slap mine
or a voice from behind reproach me for sneaking
inside what had been for days your private space.

But the morning sun cast a pattern of light –
long rectangles from the half-opened shutters –
and I felt welcomed by its warmth, stepped further across
the boards which had creaked your arrival so often before,
allowed me now the chance to tinker where dust motes fell.

There had been others before, their pictures framed –
proud black dancer with bare breasts and in a tiny twenties
gouache, three figures climbing up a hill of Sussex snow;
O, there were flowers in Storrington,
on the turf and on the spray.

Now a robin lands on the granite sill, a mouse finds its way
up through gaps in the wooden floor, feasts on apple cores
left in the week's bin and late September flies rise up
from the still lake, bounce bumbling off the glass.
This room will have its way, with or without us.

Nights of secret fluorescent paint, lighting up installation slate.
Nights of the swinging pink-red door, its ancient laundry list
still pasted there linen sheets, bolster covers, servants' blankets …
Nights of bats flitting from the eaves above the window ledge,
nights of the foxes screaming on the half-moon lawn below.

Morning sun, its carpet of light – the mahogany handle turns.
I've come to your room and you are gone.
With or without us, this room will have its way.
O, there were flowers in Storrington,
on the turf and on the spray.

Cabin in the Woods

for Sam

There's the Doberman –
as startled by us
as we are by her,
standing hip-high
in the damp black grass.

There's the cabin
with its rain tank,
its wood pellet stove,
its solar lights
and bamboo walls.

There are yesterday's
ghosts chattering
like magpies
and there's the forest
of mud paths.

In the plots close by
the young trees sigh
their late summer sighs
and lights are draped
like washing over the terrace.

And there's us –
wild haired,
with dirty finger nails.
We're city guests
awed by the quiet.

Then sleep comes,
night's fox
is chased away
and morning is the dog
that scratches at our door.

Last Painting

in memory of Ulla

At night
the solar lamp
circles the land
like the witches'
marks of infinity
we found chalked
on the forest floor.

The Milky Way
scatters overhead
and night lays
down its booty –
the far-off cars
on the motorway,
the hoot of a barn owl,

the small girl dreaming
her knee in your back,
one foolish hen asleep
in the Doberman's hut,
the red boats still bobbing
on your last painting,
the easel dusty now –

then the light goes out.

Text

I wake to your words
falling with the rain
and cup them in my hand.
Such short, simple things
with no punctuation
to bind them tight
and yet their meaning
is caught in the flow
of thought on the screen.
A beep and I reply,
imagining your hands,
somewhere else,
reaching up to catch
my words back to you.
A house destroyed,
a river path overgrown,
conservatory glass
all shattered, a walled
garden locked, the past
drowning, but this text
grasps at the future,
is what was and cannot ·
be forgotten.

4 a.m.

after reading Wislawa Szymborska

No one feels good
at four in the morning.
Even the fox has given up
its search at Gort na Cille,
has surrendered to the lane's
steel trap, its straw and bait
that was always there
waiting for him in the ditch.

The bulb of hope has blown,
can never be replaced again.
But then light chases
shadows away up the hill,
over waking ticks
and rustling mice,
the triumphant buzzard,
a thrush in its beak.

It's five in the morning.
The lost kitten has nestled
back into her sleep.
The slippers by the bed's edge
are stepped into one more time.
The shutters open. Morning hums.
And there is always the surprise
of your hand reaching to touch my face.

Under the Tree

for Ciarán Farrell

Then the big sun rose, trouncing winter.
Everything was possible and we spoke
under the tree – Beethoven, Mozart –
names like secrets we'd just
dragged from the hushed lake.

We who had come from the cabin
in the woods, where the grate
was always bare, the pot cold,
the jar empty, but who'd tugged
from our pockets the angel, carved

from amethyst, that our fathers
taught us to raise high –
pink talisman to fight off
the wolves of hunger and fear.
They would not have their way.

And though our bellies ached,
we trudged on, found at last the path
by that grey-green lake where the sun
steadied, everything was possible and we
stood under the beech speaking of them.

Hunting Dogs, Hares and Frogs

Late September
and I'd left my desk
to stroll by the lake,
the orange path
crunching underfoot,
the air grown clear
from a risen mist.

Then the hoarse alarm
of a jackdaw's *kaaaarr,*
and I heard them howl,
those hunting dogs come
after work, chasing
the hares through
the forest dark.

Out onto the rolling green
the petrified hares came
preparing to drown
themselves in fear.
But the frogs, afraid
of them, leapt into
the dense lake first.

And I remembered
the fable –
By the water's edge
the wise hare knows
there's always
someone
worse off than him

Three Visitors

came to my house.
Three travellers

weary from what
went before.

*I didn't think a lot
about the journey,*

the first one said,
until I was half-way there.

I didn't realise,
the second one sighed,

*how much more
was possible.*

It seems too late now,
the last one said.

And yet, all three agreed,
You have opened

*your door to us,
the room is well lit,*

*the smell of food
rises from the table,*

and from sleep
will surely come,

the privilege
of a new moment.

NOTES

'Time Capsule' refers to *Dearcán na nDaoine / The People's Acorn*, a sculpture project for Áras an Uachtaráin by artist Rachel Joynt. Dreams and wishes from people aged 4 to 94 throughout Ireland, written in writing workshops conducted by the author, were collected and preserved in a time capsule within the sculpture, to remain unopened for one hundred years. President Michael D. Higgins unveiled *The People's Acorn* on December 14th, 2107.

'The Ledger' is inspired by a collection of poems by Peter Sirr, *The Ledger of Fruitful Exchange* (The Gallery Press, 1995), with its cover painting, 'Self Portrait with his Wife, Anna Maria' (c. 1800) by Robert Fagan.

'Speed's Map' refers to John Speed's map of Dublin, 1610, which is the first known map of the city.

'Private Space' makes use of a quote from the poem 'Daisy' by the English Poet Francis Thompson (1859–1907):

> *O, there were flowers in Storrington,*
> *on the turf and on the spray.*